where do we go from here?

Angelica Ashley

Copyright © 2025 Angelica Ashley Epino

All rights reserved. No part of this book may be reproduced or used in any matter without written permission of the copyright owner except for the use of quotations in a book review.

Other Books Written by
Angelica Ashley

All The Girls Beau Loved

you can't save her

Unhinged Honesty

Is This What Happy Looks Like?

To my editor,

I love you.

The day I decide to love you, that's it.

What I give now is what I'll give forever.

I will not stop loving you until you tell me to stop.

Even then, I don't know if I could.

The day my heart and mind decides you're the one, they'll never let go.

So, we'll take it all day by day,

And I'll love you like there's no tomorrow,

Just in case.

/day by day/

I wish I could keep you

I wish I could call you mine

I want to believe I'd be a good mother

I played pretend when I was nine

That's no good, that's not enough

I wasn't planning on that second line

He'll hold my hand as I say goodbye

I'll ask forgiveness from the divine

In my heart, there's a tally I keep secret

You'll be that second line

/that second line/

You were the last person on my mind. You were the last person I ever thought I'd feel this way about. You drive me insane. It doesn't make sense for this to make sense, but it does. It does make sense.

You are the last person on my mind before I go to sleep.

You are the last person I'd choose and you will be.

No better choice for me than you.

/the last person/

I keep finding myself in the hands of someone who doesn't know if they are capable of love.

I have this unwarranted belief that I can love enough for the both of us.

My heart is the barrel in the backyard collecting rainwater.

I keep forgetting that no matter how big a bucket is, it can still be emptied.

/the bucket/

I want to love you completely without fear and without nervousness, but I can hear the glass shards of my heart scrape against each other as it tries to beat for you. The bandages tear and rip as my heart pushes itself to work. It hurts to love now. It fights so hard, but it's tired and it's on its last strands.

If this doesn't work,

I'm not sure it'll survive it.

/the patchwork heart/

I am the sun

You shield your face

You avert your eyes

I hope I blind you

I hope you never see me again

Yet I hope you can never escape my image

I hope my beautiful amazing wonderful life

Haunts your sad existence

I hope I'm the ghost in your periphery around every corner you pass

My work on a book shelf in every house you visit

My name on the lips of every person you meet

My words quoted by every girl who will reject your advances

My blood on your hands forever
stained by your worst sins

I am the sun

I rose again

You will never escape me

But I am free from you

/I am the sun, you will burn/

Do you understand them now?

Do you get why they yelled?

Do you get why they left?

There are demons that linger

So pour the salt on the window sill

I'll teach you all my prayers

When my hands start to scratch at my arms and neck remembering the bounds that held me down, you take them into yours.

Tell me to look into your eyes
"Breathe in deep,
you're here with me"

the darkness looms
I pray through sobs
My eyes swelling and sore

Still, I listen
I look into yours
I breathe and we survive it

/all the difficulties that come with caring for me/

You clean the windows
I can see everything clearly
You explain the best ways how
While you hold my face dearly

You visit and read me books
You show me how to cook and clean
You teach me things I didn't know
You do this all without being mean

I was left alone
Taught to wait for rescue
Never taught to care for a home
Never had one 'til you

You leave to go back to yours
I sit and feel peace in my room
I sleep and dream of our life
Finally free from all the gloom

/the caretaker's visits/

I'd stay up all night with you
asleep on my chest just so I could
make sure you slept all the way to
morning.

/sleep on me/

I've imagined my life without this relationship.

I have looked both ways

I am happy with or without us being together.

If we never took the chance, we would've been fine never knowing what we know now.

But now that I do, I don't want to know the alternative.

You do not complete me, but you add so much.

I may have been happy in both versions I looked at,

But I know I am the happiest in this one.

/there's only one way I want this life to go/

I hope curiosity catches up with you

Find my books and read what I wrote

Feel every ounce of pain and regret

Let the ink stain your heart with the darkness

you cursed upon me so long ago

My hope has become that

If I write everything down

Until there is nothing left in me

It can all be returned to you.

You can carry all that

You laid on top of me.

/that heaviness you feel on your chest when you try to sleep at night/

Tomorrow is a promise

We will forever look forward to

Tomorrow I will love you

The same way I loved you today

You'll be there waiting with a smile

A tear in your eye

A handkerchief in your pocket

Your best friend by your side

Tomorrow I will meet you there

At the end of the aisle

Tomorrow is already the best day

Tomorrow I'll get to be with you

/I'll see you tomorrow/

I loved you so much

I loved you thinking you'd be the only one I'd ever love

I gave you

all of it

all of me

everything

each time someone new attempts to love me the way I wanted you to

your touch lingers like bruises that refuse to heal

when different hands hold this body, I wince

I keep the lights on so I can see his face and know its him and not you

Your eyes darkened as you pushed me against the walls of the tower

My voice begging in whimpers unable to speak up against your words telling me what I wanted.

Your eyes black,

You are the demon

Who broke me, my heart, and my soul.

You haunt my days and nights.

You heard news of my new home, the new garden, and the new caretaker.

You do not get to be angry at the kind man

Who cares and carries my body to bed

When I find myself too weak to walk

From fighting the cruel curse

You placed upon me

Will I ever be capable of loving the way I loved you?

Am I truly cursed?

Never to fall in love?

Never to trust?

Never to give myself completely?

I escaped the tower.

Will I ever be freed from this?

/the princess' curse/

I want to crawl into the arms of someone already asleep in our bed

I want to wake up and smile because I get another day with them.

I want them to make us tea.

I want us to sit outside in the morning.

I want to tell them every thought in my mind knowing that they accept me for all I am and all I am not.

I want to be loved so deeply that "love" is not good enough of a word to describe it.

/I want to be with you for the rest of my days/

I think I'd prefer being loved on purpose

Fuck feelings

Love me with intention

/intent/

Before I leave

I always ask one more time

"do you want to stay?"

Even if I'm so tired and done with it all.

"do you want to stay?"

I will always ask before I go

I need to know that you mean it

"do you want to stay?"

This is what you want?

It's over for real this time?

"do you want to stay?"

I need you to give up on us

Because I can never say what needs to be said.

                        "no."

/one last question and one last answer/

When the kisses get softer and more mundane

When the hands aren't as sweaty as they used to be

When the heart slows instead of speeds

/that's when you know/

I once read that when you like someone you should just befriend them instead of dating.

So you can keep them forever.

When we decided to become a couple and pursue a committed relationship, I found myself fearing that a mistake was being made.

A mistake that couldn't be undone and that I've foolishly doomed myself again to lose another person I wouldn't know what to do without.

But then you ask me to look into your green eyes, and you say "where have I been the last few years? Haven't I been right here? Why would I ever leave you now?"

I stare blankly as my mind attempts to take me away.

"I want this. I asked you because I want you."

Your words reach up and pull me back down and into your arms.

"You are safe. I know you don't know what's next. I promise you won't have to find out alone."

/where do we go from here?/

I used to hate myself for leaving

Carrying around guilt for abandoning you

For abandoning us

The truth of it is that

I don't believe I've ever left

I'm still in the same place

The tower

The café

The forest

The garden

This house

They are all one and the same

Redecorated to fit my newest fantasy until it fades

But it's important to note that

You were never the person I stayed for

There is a little girl who plays in the garden.

She was left behind

Cursed to wander this land

Searching for the ghost of a coward

we often find her asleep among the flowers

the caretaker now cradles her in his arms

I watch him care for her with a gentleness she's never known till now

/she is everything to him/

If I ever lose myself again
I know where to find her
In the darkness, in the night,
In the mud, in the ashes

She's crawling to where you exist

Even when she knows nothing,
She knows you,

/wherever you are/

Will you get down on your knee for me?

Will you cry when I walk down the aisle?

Will you hold my hand as we wait for the two minute timer to ring?

Will you wash the dishes?

Will you wake in the middle of the night to soothe a crying baby?

Will you stay by my side at my mother's funeral?

Will you bring me food when I can't leave the bed?

Will you wear a tutu and play tea party with our daughter?

Will you celebrate each and every time we find out?

Will you teach our son to play ball?

Will you carry me out when I bleed and stain the mattress?

Will you call your sister to watch our daughter for the night?

Will you drive the car?

Will you sit by bedside?

Will you hold my hand as we wait for it to be over?

Will you forgive me?

Will you forgive me?

Will you forgive me?

Will you forgive me?

Will you forgive me?

Will you forgive me?

Will you forgive me?

/thick and thin/

"Its always about you. The last four years, everything I've done has been for you. What you want. What you need. It's all you, you, you."

I wanted so badly to slap him in that moment.

How dare he say those words to me?

I don't think i ever asked for anything i didn't deserve

In fact, i think i was under asking if anything.

If that was him doing everything for me,

Then why was it that i had to beg for him

To spend time with me

To hug me

To tell me nice things

Basic acts of affection and kindness

Why is it such a chore to love me?

It was so easy for me to love you

I listened and did the things you asked

I only called every other day when you said you thought calling every night was unnecessary

I gave up on my dreams of marriage and motherhood when you said you didn't want to get married or have kids

I held you when you cried when your dad sold the motorcycle you were so close to fixing, but you said you didn't have the energy to deal with me when i would have panic attacks in the middle of the night after my cat died in the very bed we were sleeping in.

I believed in you, that you would be a good man, but i don't think a good man would treat me the way you did.

You may have been better than the exe before you, but that wasn't a very high bar to beat.

You didn't physically harm me, wow, would you like a trophy?

I don't know you.

I thought I did. But I didn't.

I wish you were a better man.

I wish you were the man i thought you were.

I wish you were more than a story i made up in my mind

It's not fair.

/I made you up, didn't i?/

Is it too much to ask for you to be kind?

I don't deserve to feel like I am less than.

I stopped eating each time you felt the need to comment on my body.

The body that others remark as beautiful,

You compare to a sack of rice.

The body I was blessed with can be found across the world and centuries in thousands of paintings and sculptures.

The body with the curves of the goddesses.

The body that would've attracted many a suitor in the regency era

The body that would've been considered controversially sexy in the 50's.

Don't you dare shame me for how I exist.

Your words shook my young mind
until it broke.

I didn't eat enough.

I ate too much.

I became nauseous from the
confusing contradictory care you
provided.

I thought it'd only help me.

Nothing helped.

I didn't need help.

Feel my body. Feel my bones.

Feel the placement of my bones.

I AM BUILT TO LOOK THIS WAY.

I WAS DESIGNED BY THE UNIVERSE

TO BE LOVED.

YOU ARE A WOMAN OF GOD.

DON'T YOU DARE QUESTION HIS
DESIGN.

I AM YOUR CHILD.

I AM HIS CHILD.

I am His child.

and you are my mother.

/PLEASE LOVE ME AS I AM/

I need a mother

I need a mother who cares.

I need a mother who loves me.

despite everything I am

Every flaw and failure.

Every time I fall

I need a mother who would pick me up and hold me instead of telling me I shouldn't have fallen in the first place and that I should've known better. I didn't know because when I asked for answers, she told me I was smarter than her and that I already know what to do.

Why would I ask if I already knew?

You wonder why I don't ask anymore.

I wonder where I was supposed to learn everything I was supposed to know when no one took the time to teach me.

I needed a mother.

I need a mother.

/dearest mother, why did you not mother me?

I'm scared to be sick
I don't want to be another person
You're afraid of losing this way
I see what you carry in your mind
I don't want to add to it

I want to take care of you
Not the other way around
I have too many plans
For this to be our reality

Maybe that's why I moved so fast

Maybe I knew my time would be short

I want to have forever with you

I will not get sick

I will tell my body to stop

To not be sick

To fix my cells

To let me stay

So I can stay with you

/my lungs will continue to breathe, just for you/

My mother taught me to forgive others as God is the only one with the power to judge.

I hug you and I say "I love you"

I walk away angry that you never gave me the same courtesy.

I walk away frustrated that every conversation became about my sister as if I'm not your daughter too.

I walk with money you borrowed from her pocket because that's all you could give me.

I walk away heartbroken at how my arms wrap just as tight around you as when I was little enough to jump into yours.

I hug you and I say "I love you"

I don't even know if I'm being truthful when I say those words.

I want to believe that I do.

But I don't know you.

You are a stranger
that I want to hug.
You are a stranger
that I wasn't to love.
You are a stranger
that I call dad.

/I will still hug you/

Seven is my favourite number

Seven is my lucky number

The Seventh of December is my birthday

But I heard that it takes on average seven times to leave an abusive situation.

Seven times I was prepared to leave us behind but ended up on my knees begging you to stay

Seven times I swore things would get better

Seven times I made myself smaller so you could hold me

Seven times you wiped my tears by pushing my face down on my mattress

Seven times the night started with sobs and ended with sex

Seven times before you finally
gave up and let me free

Seven times before you listened to
your own words and left knowing I
deserved more than what you could
give me.

/seven/

I AM MORE THAN CAPABLE
OF CREATING A WONDERFUL LIFE
FOR MYSELF.

I CAN SEE THAT EVERYTHING I WANT
IS ALREADY MINE.

I AM ALL THAT I HAVE EVER NEEDED.
I AM ALL THAT I HAVE EVER WANTED.

/a thank you note to myself/

Everything I've said
has been said before
I have always known
I am nothing new
The universe works in a way
Where sometimes messages
have to find you.

So, if I merely exist to say
Something blue is blue,
I hope that you read it
I hope you find meaning in it

I hope that you know my words are true.

/angelica/

We went to the park today

He took a break out of his busy day to go for a walk.

I told him how I'm still sad

I don't know if I'll ever be happy

No matter how much he tries

It might never happen

I feel bad for making him care

I'm sorry for everything

He kissed me on the forehead

Held me as my eyes dripped water

He told me all the reasons

He'll still keep trying

Happy is one of the goals,

But it isn't the main one

The goals are to
keep getting to see me
keep moving forward
keep living

He told me
He sees how hard I'm working
He sees how fast I'm running
toward my dreams
he worries I'll leave him behind

I tell him
I never want to leave him
I will do my best to never leave

/I will do my best/

I know if I never spoke again

You'd sit in waiting for the words to return

You'd never tell me you were

You would never make me feel bad for being quiet

You'd just hold my hands

You'd kiss me on the forehead

You'd hold me in your arms

You'd carry me to safety

You'd do anything to keep me safe

Even if I never moved again

You'd still love me if I became a statue

You'd put me somewhere safe

You'd sit with me

You'd tell me about your day

You'd wash me

You'd dust me

You'd let no one else touch me

My hands and my forehead

would shine almost golden

from your habits persisting

/the caretaker's most precious
thing/

I work night shifts now

I often think about you

When it's 2 am and I'm on my break

I hope that you're sleeping soundly so you can survive school in the morning

I hope you wake up rested and happy that you're awake once more

I hope when my hours are up

and I get to go home,

I'll get to go home to you

/night shift/

I am the forest

I have no map of this place

I am so scared

I wonder if it shows on my face

The ribbon around my neck

Feels more like rope than lace

Both blind in the dark

Do not trip, keep a steady pace

/hold my hand and do not let go/

I don't feel quite like a person

I just seem to inhabit a body

A body that just doesn't always

Feel like it is mine

A ghost playing pretend

Maybe I died so long ago

Took the body as a host

I can't remember

I stole it

This life

It was meant for someone else

Someone better

I haunt my own life

Floating

Wandering

Barely here

/apparition/

Even the kindest men are still men. They will never understand the feeling of knowing the world doesn't care. It is so much deeper than a fucked up election. It is a world that doesn't care enough to fight for us. Our safety. Our rights. Our needs. One of the most powerful and influential countries in the world has decided that women are not important. They do not know anything. Uneducated and unwilling to be educated.

Predators get away

Disgusting acts of violence are cheered for

Rape is being excused

Overlooked

Forgotten

Even the kindest men need to be better

There is an ongoing fight for woman's lives

Either you are with us or not

There is no inbetween.

Tired of teaching

Tired of explaining empathy to egotistical idiots ending endless lives with their choices

I fear Canada will follow

I am tired. So very tired.

I shouldn't be scared

To be a woman

To be brown

To be alive

/I should want to stay alive/

This.

This night

I am blind.

I am wandering in the dark

My trachea shattered

By his hands

I try to push the monster away,

But he's warm

I feel the blood drain

from my face

its rushes out my chest

the dagger sunk deep

my blood is warm

I want so badly to run

The wind howls

The snow falls heavy

I am weak and dying

at least, I am warm

/why did you stay so long?/

He's started to dream now

He shares his ideas

Of a house

The kids running around it

The babies they began as

My stomach housing them first

It is strange

I've had the wonderful privilege

Of watching him fall in love

/he's finally caught up/

My bank account has money in it

I know that should be something obvious

That's not been my experience

I've spent my life learning how to balance it

Moving money around to not get in a mess with the masters

My mind and its many mental illnesses have an affinity for overspending when sad

Self-control and setting cash aside are skills I still study

With my life starting to calm, the call of my credit cards quiet

No longer am I cowering due to their height

My debt will be repaid, I promise

Not to the companies I owe

But to the young woman who not only dug herself into the pit she's in but also caused the mountain she must climb

/slowly, but surely, we'll get out of the mud/

Sometimes I worry if the sentences I say make sense

To be truthful,

the tumble of my tongue

terrifies me so much

I tremble

Unless uniqueness is of the utmost importance to you

Very well, if my veracity is viewed as valiant

We will not wait to write what we witness

Wishing to be xanthic

Rejecting the xeroxed ideals despite the pain radiating from the xiphoid

Thoughts zoom, zip, and zig-zag through my zealous brain.

/Sometimes I worry my sentences do not make sense/

I feel safe enough to get angry

I feel safe enough to say what I feel when I feel it

I feel safe enough to be angry

I feel safe enough to say what happened and how much it hurt me

I feel safe enough to have anger

I feel safe enough to set it down

No longer feel the need

to carry it with me anymore

/my anger isn't dangerous/

I'm the little girl who hides in her closet

seeking solace in simple solutions

Just run away, little girl

Happiness scares you, doesn't it?

The green in his eyes remind you too much of the trees dancing on a sunny windy day

That day that you knew you were falling in love with him

As he held you close and told you he'll do his best to make you as happy as possible

I'm the little girl who hides in her closet

something sinister stays silent inside her

It quiets when I hide away

I want him to know but I don't want to scare him

He is brave and strong

I know he can handle it all

I don't want him to have to

I wish I was easier to care for

I wish we could have met before

Right now, I'll listen to his words through the closed door

He's the little boy not afraid of the monster in the closet

But of the world outside

Simply seeking the same solace in her arms

/the monster in the closet/

I've been so many different versions of myself

All at one

Acting different from how I feel

Trying to make everyone around me feel better than myself

The roles I carry contradict each other

They pull me apart 'til I tear like a ballgown through a crowded and narrow forest path

I wish to only exist as one

One role to fulfill

I wish to just be myself

I wish that could be enough for me.

/me, myself, and i/

He makes me feel so tiny and small

Not in the way you did

He makes me feel so fragile and delicate

Not in the way you did

He does it in a way that I feel safe enough to jump into his arms knowing he'll never drop me

/I am easy to carry because he is easy to hold/

The date of your return

Now gone and past

My heart in the hands of another

May he be the last

To you, my first

May we never meet again

I say goodbye to you

And to all the pain

/October 21ˢᵗ, 2024/

Maybe it wasn't a bucket of blood

But a tap dripping

You laid the towel over my face

I couldn't see as you started ripping my dress

My thighs left sore from your gripping

Did you think it was beautiful?

That body you were stripping

She found herself in the garden

Her mind slowly slipping

There she wanders away

There she wanders away

/surviving torture/

Everything is changing
And I know that
It doesn't scare me anymore
I'm ready to go
You have changed my life
There are so many paths I can take
So, with your hand in mine
I only have one question left

Where do we go from here?

/my greatest adventure begins/

I've been asking myself

"what is the purpose of my life?"

I was supposed to be something.

Something worthy.

When my heart would break,

I'd tell myself

"there's a reason for this. This is just preparing me. This is nothing but a trial to prove that you are the one. The one special wonderful thing that everyone has been waiting for. It's you. So, you have to stay alive to find out what it is. This incredible reason you exist. You were born to do something. Right?"

The question mark got stronger and more emphasized as the years went on and the list of heartbreaks grew.

Until you.

You and the days I get to spend with you

Make it all make sense

Each laugh, each tear, each beautiful moment I get to have in this life is my purpose

I exist to be alive and live

/sometimes it's the simplest answer/

I call every morning

A heavy weight is lifted off my chest

When I hear your voice

"Good morning, my love"

It is indeed

Knowing I get another day with you

I can begin

/wake up call/

A hall of mirrors

I see her in every one

She is a stranger

A false version

endless glass breaking

from my screams

I leap through, letting the
leftover shards slice my skin

Knowing the lines will heal

She is there

We fall to the glittering ground

Our eyes connect

"I want to be you," we say in sync

/the girl in the mirror/

I used to have this reoccurring dream of being rushed down a hospital hallway in labour with my first baby.

There was always a man with me. His face was never visible. It was blurred out, but I knew he was blond. I knew he was the love of my life. He stayed by my side the entire time until our baby was laying on my chest. He kissed me and that is when I would always wake up.

I had many crushes, mostly blonds. Hoping they could be him.

My first boyfriend wasn't, but I let it go because I was so sure that this brown-haired boy was my one true love.

After he broke me, I looked to the dream again.

My second boyfriend was blond at the start. His hair darkened as the years we were together went by. He was so close to being him. I held on so long, he was blond. He's the right one. I got it right this time. Right?

Then when we met, I didn't pay attention to your hair.

I was still with the blond turned brunet. Still trying to prove to myself and everyone around me that he was the one.

I felt so drawn to you.

I knew we would be friends.

You always wore a hat.

Every time, we spend time together as acquaintances turning to friends turning to best friends,

You had your favourite hat on.

I told you my story

and you listened.

You shared your fears

and I wiped your tears

we were a safe space

for each other.

Nothing more, nothing less

When the time came that the boy with the darkened hair left,

you had become a trusted person.

Months of moving forward

came and went.

The comfort of our friendship turned into something new.

You took your hat off to kiss me.

I had seen your hair before.

It just hadn't hit until that moment how blond it was.

In the sunshine,

it only gets lighter.

/the man of my dreams/

If I could will away all your
worries, I would

/the things you say III/

The difference between someone wanting to love you and someone who just does is one of the most painful, yet important clarifications one can learn.

I love you and I know that because I still care. I still care about you. I think about you everyday. I worry about how you feel and how you're doing. If you've eaten. If you've taken your meds. I check your facebook page just to make sure you're still alive.

I love you.

I want to stay and take care of you.

You don't love me the same way. You don't care about me unless I do what you want.

I'm not allowed to feel anything other than grateful.

You can be upset with me but I can't be upset with you.

If I treated you with the same respect, you give me, you'd say I was evil.

I've lived my life trying my best to live up to the name you gave me.

I was so young, and you designated me as your healer, your caretaker, your only hope.

I was your perfect angel.

You once said your favourite version of me was when I was a baby.

When I couldn't talk.

When I couldn't teach you the things you were supposed to teach me like how to communicate.

You taught me to hide in the dark and pray to your God who was kind enough to give me life.

Life He gave me through your womb.

A life I should be grateful to have.

I should bend down and kiss your feet.

I know you want to love me.

I know you want me to be a daughter you can love.

The child you wanted died

I took their place.

Nothing I could ever become

will be good enough for you.

You want me to return home,

but you never built a home worth returning to.

I understand you more than most.

~~I am like you.~~

I will not let myself be like you.

I will leave.

I will change.

I will grow.

I will be healthy.

/I talk to God and I ask Him to look after you because I can't do it anymore/

There once was a goddess

who would visit my tower

she'd share stories about vampires and witches and the evil that lurks and pretends to be kind

she was someone I trusted

she was my friend

but she hasn't visited since the spring

/the winter is very cold without her/

Today, I tried to reorganize my things.

It is almost 2am.

I cannot sleep.

I just have this feeling that my body will fail me and I will not rise when the sun does.

I hold my childhood teddy bear and the baby blanket I knit for my future son.

It hurts to be holding

the past I will never get back and the future I will never get.

I do not believe in hoping for a better tomorrow.

In this moment as this red pen drags itself across this page

My hand cramps painfully

I do not believe in a better tomorrow

I used to

Now, I am in the future I used to dream about

I am not happy

I am starting to think maybe it was never the situation, or the house, or the people.

It was me.

I am the problem.

There is no fix.

I will forever be alone.

The idea of dying tonight isn't the worst thought I've had

It could be the best choice.

Just quietly

No other input.

There's no one else here

In the name of me, myself, and I, I will sit so still.

/the freedom to die alone/

The little girl inside me is screaming and crying for you to pick her up and hold her.

I rarely saw you, when I did,

I just held on

I wrapped my arms around you

I clung on

Like I wish I could've when I was four

Wishing that my tiny frame would weight you down so you would never leave

There are glimpses of a relationship we could've had

You cooked my favourite food

When I would visit

You bought me things and tried to make me happy with money and material things

I think you misunderstood me

We don't know each other

You think that's all I want

I don't know how to ask for all that time with you back

I don't know how to look into your eyes and say

I wish you held me in your arms a little bit longer

/I grew up sitting on the floor waiting for you to come back and pick me up/

I melt in your arms

Your embrace is my chrysalis

I am changing

I am new

/a beautiful butterfly/

I have always felt so lonely

I never questioned why

It was a guarantee

I thought it was just one of those things

like lumps of sugar in tea

It is how it is

I did have fears about if the loneliness left too,

What would I be without my one constant?

So I just continued to sit in it alone.

Until you took me in.

As you place the mug with the bunny ears on it on the table in front of me, filled with peppermint tea.

As you fill up yours, your sister's, your mom's, and your dad's,

I sit holding my heart inside my chest,

I was wrong to be afraid, loneliness can leave me too,

It will be okay.

/As long as it leaves me with you/

I have the nicest conversations
with your mother

Her mind is filled with knowledge,
but still so curious and open to
what I have to say.

Her kindness comforts me and I
know where you learned yours.

Her eyes show patience and a lack
of judgment I've never known.

I have the nicest conversations
with your mother.

I wish she were my own

/Your mother/

<u>the reason I feel I have failed</u>

I am a mere twenty years old and I feel as if I have wasted my time. I don't believe in my own dreams, so who will? I am so lost. But there is no one to run to. My mother tells me, "you've always been smarter than me, you'll figure it out. What if I don't? what will you do then? My dearest mother, if my mind is lost, where will we find ourselves? I love you

<u>The reason I care ~~still~~ so much</u>

That little girl waiting by the window

Falling asleep in the moonlight

Hoping each car that passes will pull in

Into the driveway, open the driver's side and reveal someone who will make my mommy happy. So young, yet so tired of the sound of my mother crying herself to sleep. Promising that I will <u>never</u> let a man make me cry like my father made her.

<u>The reason I lost</u>

I let a ~~man~~ make me cry like mother cried for him. A ~~man~~ not worthy of my pain. he was a simple human boy with no idea of how to care for the girl he found. He saw right through her. Nothing about her and her fault lines and cracks and labels plastered all around her. There was no reason for failure on his side of things. He knew. He was warned over and over. DO NOT BREAK. FRAGILE. DELICATE. Yet, as all things he did, he did half-assed and careless. Disregarding the labels and warnings. THIS IS NOT A TOY. He played with the girl. Until she broke.

Of course, what else was supposed to happen?

the question I can't seem to find an answer to is, who is to blame for the broken girl? the people who made her out of glass, making her destiny to break? Or is it the reckless who didn't listen to simple instructions? Or is it the girl herself? For still choosing to believe in the idea of love, even after years of waiting by a window, with nothing to ever show for it, other than cracks and anger and failure

<u>What is the reason?</u>

I guess, we will have to live without ever knowing. The girl of glass will have to keep waiting a little longer.

/I used a typewriter I bought at the thrift store/

My socks have holes

My feet are scarred

I have walked so far

The glass shards were never cleaned up

This place exists exactly how I left it

Even is the same except

I see the plants have taken over

The wall you built is covered with green

Fruit and flowers have grown through the destruction

I pick a pear

I appreciate it's sweetness

I say thank you to the tree for it's resilience

"I remember planting you. You were mine to care for. I'm sorry for leaving you behind here. I'm sorry for not coming back when you needed me. I'm so sorry for the wreckage that surrounds you.

You grew up without me. You made something sweet and were kind enough to give it to me. Thank you, my friend.

/what a pretty pear you've picked/

You cannot take care of others
If you are not taken care of.
You cannot save others
If you are not safe.
You cannot give to others
If you have nothing to give

/no more self sacrifice/

The elite entities existing with the ability to save us

are hoarders

There is no supply of compassion

A demand for revolution

Kill the rich and eat their overstuffed bodies bloated from belligerence, just avoid the brains

Rip them to shreds and give them to the pigs

/They'll eat anything/

I am so lost in the forest

I have always been running

Never stopping to see what was here

The trees breathe with me as I walk through the deepest shades of green

I created this world and never once explored .

It was never safe to simply walk before.

/I've created something beautiful/

I went to visit my old tower

The first one where I grew up

Flowers have taken over The surrounding garden of fixed figures

When I was younger

My mother would talk about how beautiful my friends were

How much more beautiful they were than me

Because they were more ladylike and poised and put in effort to be pretty

I loved my friends for how kind they were and how much fun we had when we'd play

But my mother would keep reminding me about how much fairer their skin was and how much more mannered they seemed

I knew them differently than what she did

She never got to know my friends like I did

I knew that they were just as messy as me.

That they were not perfect.

That is why I loved them.

My mother's constant comparisons cursed them to be statues of perfection.

Each and every one placed on a pedestal.

They were always out of reach.

Now I return

standing taller

I can see them more clearly

They are reaching out to me the same way I reach for them

I was never lesser nor were they ever more.

/my mother has eyes like medusa/

I'm so scared of succeeding so sing self-sabotage with me

The perfect solution for sluts with issues committing.

Sending terrible tearful texts to their exes and screenshots of said texts to their soulmate

Whining while wincing

At every slurred word

Trying to explain why you needed to send it in the first place

Scared you screwed this up for the sixth time

/Sometimes you are the problem/

I still see you around

You are no longer a source of fear

More a hindrance

I question, "why are you here?"

You, so small and weak and lurking

I see you over there

Go away already

I am so tired of your leer

I told the kingdom of your sins

So my now guarded gardens you should steer clear

/starting to disappear/

The caretaker considered moving into my cottage

It was not the right time

His home needs him longer than he thought

I visit his home often, and he visits mine the same

I miss him terribly when we part

But I know his house needs it's heart

/get home safe, my dearest darling/

Where am I trying to go?

Do I really want the fame that forces you to hide away from the public?

Worry each day about the safety of

Friends and family

Let the critics take hold of your brain

Turn this beautiful method of healing into a factory of false authenticity and lie about rehabilitation

I am so scared to be found

That this beautiful forest I've created in my mind might become colonized by greed

Influenced by the markets filled with multiple booths selling the same plastic items to tired parents with whining children

I fear veering away from the path I set on here

Whispers of money-making schemes

Haunt me in a maternal voice

I wish I could survive on my words alone

No need for a full-time job or a dream of a self-sustaining bookshop

I would like to live a life not worried about my most basic needs

I am writing this on my 30min lunch break at my 3 dollars above minimum wage job.

I work 40 hours a week and I still do not make enough to be able to save.

I swear if I do not scream and shout about being seen, I will be stuck where I am and suffer living paycheck to paycheck.

I know I am luckier than most.

But to be grateful for survival is a given

I will save my contentment for when I am comfortable

If better if possible, I will claw my way out of the dirt

The world rewards the wicked

The kind are left to fend for each other

The systems were built to keep us down

But we must all push against the walls

Each brick taken works towards the tumble of the tower

Keep true and kindness can win

/they will all come tumbling down/

Those who have not experienced the world through your skin and suffering do not have a say on how you survive

/tell them all to shut the fuck up/

Everyone I love wants to leave this place

Venture far away

Somewhere where it's nicer and prettier and just better than anything we have here

It seems I am the simpleton

The only one stupid enough to want to stay

I want to build a home

To keep a house

To live somewhere long enough that I can truly say I lived there

I've been told I have a talent for nesting

Making even the shittiest shoebox cozy instead of cramped

But they will still snicker behind my back

Judging my home by it's imperfections

But they do not understand

It is not a skill or a talent to make somewhere unhomely home

It is a tactic of survival

I will find shelter wherever I can

I am desperate for warmth

Let me cover up the black mold on the edges of my windows with curtains that match

Let my cat hunt the mice

I am so tired of forgiving

I am so tired of adapting

My hands are peeling from scrubbing this place clean

It is not my house

It is not my home.

/I want a place to call my own/

I worry that my work is a bit too simple

That my books are nothing more than just a quick read or something aesthetic to have on a neatly designed bookshelf in a teen girls room

That is part of the dream

But if you wanted me to tell the honest truth

I do not know if my work is worth the money you spent on this book

I do not know if you get as much as I do out of this book's existence.

I want this book to mean something to you but I have no idea who you are

Or what you need from this.

My words playing in your mind trying to figure out if I can figure out where I am going with all of this.

The answer is nowhere.

I write words down the same way I
think of them.

I only hope that someone reads
this and figures out something
really important

Something that only reading this
book would allow them to realize.

The words you need to read will
find their way to you

/Is anyone reading this?/

Thank you for reading my book.

- Angelica Ashley <3

www.ingramcontent.com/pod-product-compliance
Lightning Source LLC
Chambersburg PA
CBHW020341010526
44119CB00048B/561